THE SPECTACULAR SCIENCE OF
PLANET EARTH

written by Rob Colson

illustrated by
Moreno Chiacchiera

KINGFISHER
LONDON & NEW YORK

KINGFISHER
LONDON & NEW YORK

First published 2023 by Kingfisher
an imprint of Macmillan Children's Books
The Smithson, 6 Briset Street,
London, EC1M 5NR
Associated companies throughout
the world
www.panmacmillan.com

EU representative: Macmillan Publishers
Ireland Limited, 1st Floor,
The Liffey Trust Centre, 117-126 Sheriff Street
Upper, Dublin 1, D01 YC43

Author: Rob Colson
Illustrator: Moreno Chiacchiera
Consultant: Penny Johnson
Designed and edited by Tall Tree Ltd

ISBN: 978-0-7534-7966-7

A CIP record for this book is available from
the Library of Congress.

Printed in China
9 8 7 6 5 4 3 2 1
1TR/0823/WKT/RV/128MA

MIX
Paper | Supporting
responsible forestry
FSC® C116313

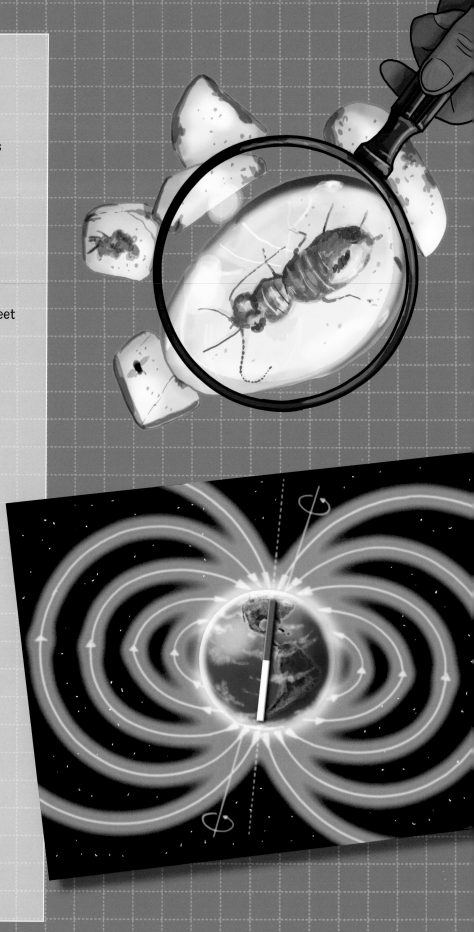

CONTENTS

INTRODUCING OUR PLANET

Earth formed 4.5 billion years ago from a swirling mass of gas and dust around the newly formed Sun. Earth is one of four rocky planets that orbit the Sun, along with Mercury, Venus, and Mars.

Crust
3–40 miles thick

EARTH'S LAYERS

Inner core
This is a solid ball made mostly of the metals iron and nickel. It has a temperature of 10,000°F, roughly the same temperature as the surface of the Sun.

Outer core
This is made of liquid iron and nickel. It has a temperature of between 8,000°F and 10,000°F. Movements of the molten metal in the outer core create Earth's magnetic field.

Mantle
This is a thick layer of silicate rock that contains two-thirds of Earth's mass. It is mostly solid, but parts of it are molten. The temperature in the mantle ranges from 7,000°F at the boundary with the outer core to 400°F at the boundary with the crust.

Crust
This is a thin shell of solid rock that surrounds the mantle. It is broken up into tectonic plates that slowly move over time (see pages 10–11).

Mantle
1,770 miles thick

MOON

The Moon is Earth's only natural satellite. Scientists think that the Moon formed a few million years after Earth when a Mars-sized planet known as Theia collided with Earth.

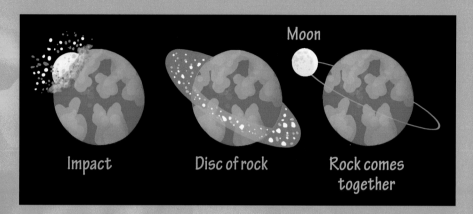

Impact   Disc of rock   Moon   Rock comes together

The impact created a disc of rock in orbit around Earth. Gravity pulled the rock together to form the Moon.

ROTATION AND ORBIT

Earth rotates on its axis once a day. The side facing toward the Sun is in daylight, while the side facing away from the Sun is in darkness. Earth orbits the Sun once a year. Earth's axis of rotation is tilted by 23.4 degrees. This tilt creates the seasons as Earth orbits the Sun.

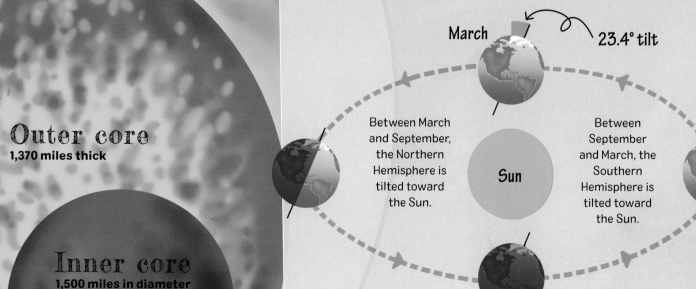

March

23.4° tilt

Between March and September, the Northern Hemisphere is tilted toward the Sun.

Sun

Between September and March, the Southern Hemisphere is tilted toward the Sun.

September

Outer core
1,370 miles thick

Inner core
1,500 miles in diameter

THE YOUNG EARTH

During its early years, our planet was a very different place from today.

HADEAN EON

Earth's first 500 million years are known as the Hadean Eon. During this time, the planet was constantly bombarded by asteroids. Rocks at the surface were solidifying, but currents in the magma brought molten rock to the surface. The surface temperature was as high as 450°F, and volcanoes dotted the fiery landscape.

FIRST LIFE

Earth's surface gradually cooled during the Hadean Eon, and a hard rocky crust formed the first continents. By the start of the Archaean Eon, which lasted from 4 billion years ago to 2.5 billion years ago, most of Earth's crust was under a deep ocean. The oldest known life forms date from the Archaean Eon. These were mats of tiny single-celled organisms, whose fossils have been found in 3.5-billion-year-old rocks. The organisms lived in shallow lakes and seas.

Stromatolites are rocky mounds that were formed by mats of microbial life 3.5 billion years ago.

Glowing orange

During the Archaean Eon, Earth would have appeared orange from space due to droplets of methane in the atmosphere. At this time, there was no oxygen gas in Earth's atmosphere.

LIVING PLANET

Life on Earth began at some point in its first billion years. It took a long time before any large lifeforms appeared, but when they did, life started to develop much more rapidly.

WHAT DOES LIFE NEED?

Nobody knows exactly how life started on Earth, but a number of conditions were needed first.

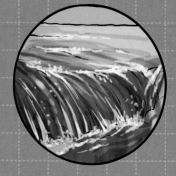

Liquid water is needed for the wide range of chemical reactions life requires.

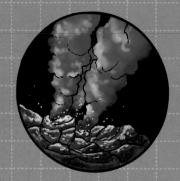

A source of energy is needed to power the chemical reactions. This comes from **the Sun** or from chemicals around **hydrothermal vents** at the bottom of the oceans.

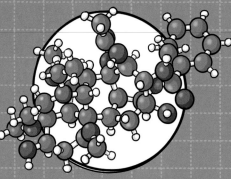

A number of key elements are needed to allow organic molecules to form. These include **carbon, nitrogen, phosphorus,** and **sulfur**.

With these conditions in place, life developed in a process called evolution.

EDIACARAN OCEANS

For billions of years, the only lifeforms on Earth were single-celled organisms. The first multicellular life evolved about 1.5 billion years ago, but large lifeforms as we know them first appeared at the start of the Ediacaran Period, 635 million years ago. Simple animals such as Charnia (left) grew on the seabeds, gently swaying in the currents and feeding on nutrients in the water. There were no predators, so creatures like Charnia had no need to protect themselves.

Aysheaia

CAMBRIAN EXPLOSION

Starting 540 million years ago, the quiet life of the Ediacaran Period changed dramatically during a period known as the Cambrian Explosion. Many kinds of new lifeforms evolved within a few million years, including the ancestors of today's animals. The first predators appeared as the oceans became more interesting places, and much more dangerous (below)!

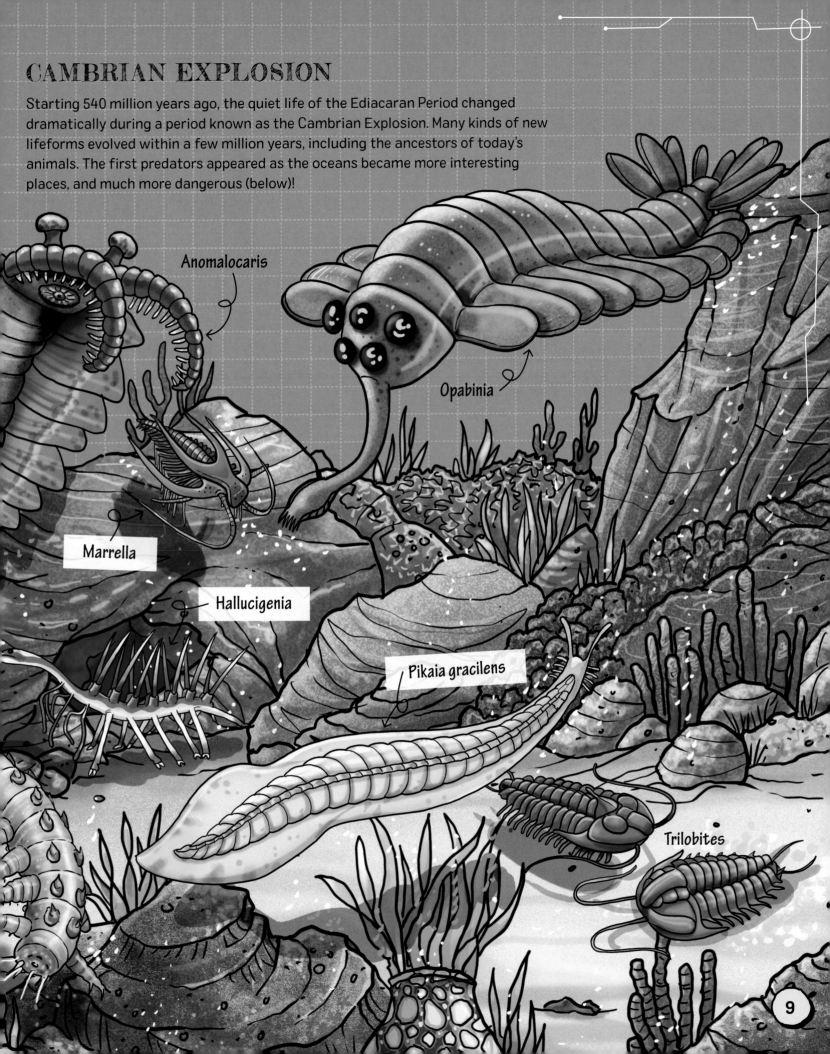

Anomalocaris

Opabinia

Marrella

Hallucigenia

Pikaia gracilens

Trilobites

SHIFTING PLATES

Earth's crust is made up of large rocky plates that fit next to each other like pieces in a huge jigsaw puzzle. These are known as tectonic plates. They sit on the mantle and move by a few centimeters each year. Over time, this movement has transformed the surface of the planet.

Types of crust

The continents are formed of continental crust. This is made mostly of the rock granite and is usually about 25 miles thick. The ocean beds are formed of oceanic crust. This is much thinner than continental crust, at about 4 miles thick. It is made mostly of the rock basalt and is about 10 percent denser than continental crust.

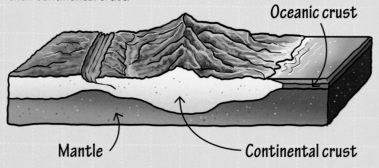

Oceanic crust

Mantle

Continental crust

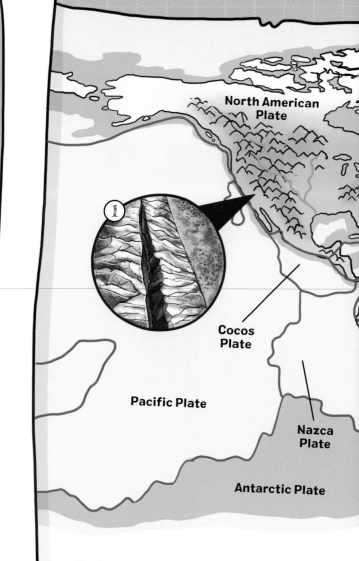

North American Plate

Cocos Plate

Pacific Plate

Nazca Plate

Antarctic Plate

1. San Andreas Fault
Located at a transform boundary between the Pacific Plate and the North American Plate, which extends through the US state of California. Frequent earthquakes occur.

PLATE BOUNDARIES

Tectonic plates meet at plate boundaries. There are three kinds of plate boundary.

Divergent boundary

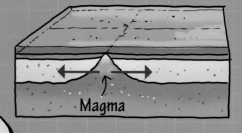

Magma

Plates are moving away from each other. Magma (molten rock) rises to the surface to form new crust in the gap and earthquakes are common.

Transform boundary

Plates are sliding past each other, creating fault valleys or undersea canyons. Earthquakes are common as the plates move in jolts.

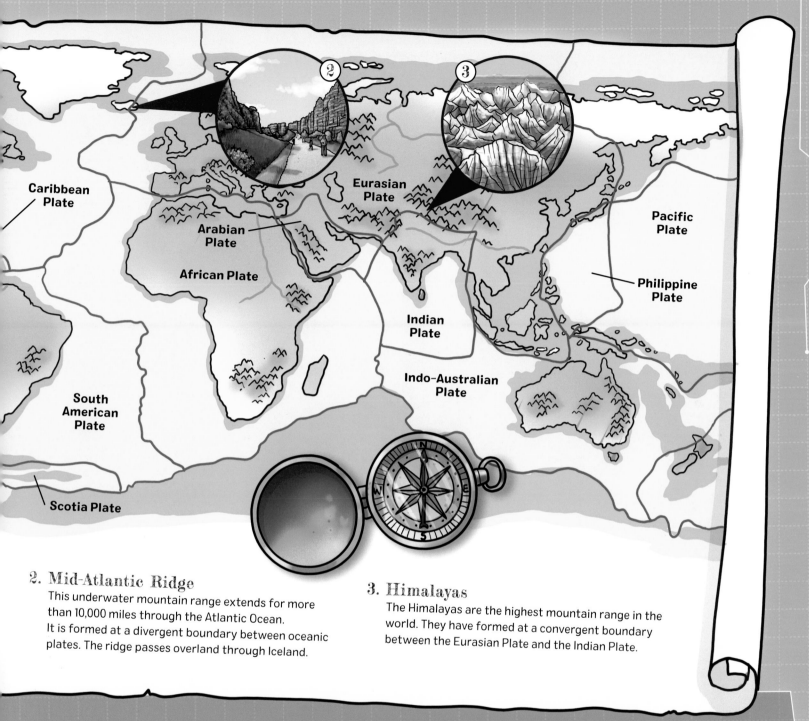

Caribbean
Plate

Arabian
Plate

African Plate

Eurasian
Plate

Pacific
Plate

Philippine
Plate

Indian
Plate

South
American
Plate

Indo-Australian
Plate

Scotia Plate

2. Mid-Atlantic Ridge

This underwater mountain range extends for more than 10,000 miles through the Atlantic Ocean. It is formed at a divergent boundary between oceanic plates. The ridge passes overland through Iceland.

3. Himalayas

The Himalayas are the highest mountain range in the world. They have formed at a convergent boundary between the Eurasian Plate and the Indian Plate.

Convergent

At convergent boundaries, plates are coming together. Where two oceanic plates converge (**1**), one of the plates is pushed down. Where two continental plates converge (**2**), both plates buckle, forming fold mountains. Where a continental plate converges with an oceanic plate (**3**), the oceanic plate bends downward. Convergent boundaries are often violent places, with strings of volcanoes and large earthquakes.

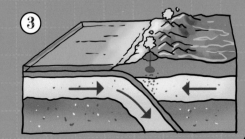

THE ANDES

Running for 5,500 miles along the western side of South America, the Andes is the longest mountain range above sea level. The Andes are made up of a series of smaller mountain ranges, or cordilleras, separated by high plateaux. They have formed at a convergent boundary between the Nazca Plate and the South American Plate.

Machu Picchu
Altiplano
Aconcagua
Cerro Torre

Aconcagua
The highest peak in the Andes, Aconcagua is located in the Principal Cordillera range. It is 22,838 feet high.

ALTIPLANO

The Altiplano is the highest plateau in South America. With an average height of 12,300 feet, much of the Altiplano is a cool desert. It is dotted with active volcanoes.

The Árbol de Piedra (Spanish for "Stone Tree") is an unusual rock formation that projects out of the Altiplano sand dunes in southern Bolivia. It was formed through erosion of the soft sandstone by sand blown by the wind.

THE IMPOSSIBLE MOUNTAIN

The jagged peak Cerro Torre in the Southern Andes is one of the hardest mountains in the world to climb. In 2012, Austrian climbers David Lama and Peter Ortner completed the first free ascent of the mountain. This means that they did not use aids such as bolts in the rock to help them to climb. Their feat had previously been described by fellow mountaineers as "crazy and impossible."

4,026 feet

David Lama

CITY IN THE MOUNTAINS

Located on a 7,970-foot-high ridge between two mountains in southern Peru are the remains of a fortified city called Machu Picchu. The city was built by the Inca in the 15th century as a mountain retreat for the emperor Pachacuti. The Inca abandoned the site about a century later, at the time that Spanish invaders were conquering their empire.

ICE AGES

Throughout our planet's history, it has cycled between warm periods in which all but the highest mountains were free of ice and cold periods in which much of the planet was covered in an ice sheet. These cold periods are known as ice ages.

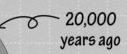

20,000 years ago

North Pole

Today

RIVERS OF ICE

Glaciers are huge rivers of ice that slowly slide down mountains to the sea. On the way, they carve out the rocks beneath them. When ice ages come to an end, the glaciers melt, leaving behind wide "U"-shaped valleys.

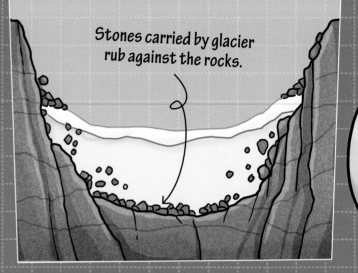

Stones carried by glacier rub against the rocks.

INTERGLACIAL

Today, we are living in a period known as an interglacial. This is a warmer period during an ice age in which glaciers retreat and the ice caps around the poles shrink in size. The colder periods are known as glacials. The current interglacial started about 20,000 years ago. As ice sheets on land melted and drained into the oceans, sea levels rose, flooding much of the land. This was a different process from the one that is causing today's global warming (see pages 42–43).

DOGGERLAND

About 8,000 years ago, as sea levels rose, an area in northwest Europe known as Doggerland was flooded. This wide strip of land connected Britain to continental Europe. It is now covered by the North Sea. Scientists have discovered the remains of plants and animals on the seabed, as well as spears and axes made by the people who roamed across the land.

9,000 years ago

Land area today

People once lived on Doggerland, hunting large animals such as mammoths.

Snowball Earth

In South Australia, geologists have discovered rocks that were left by glaciers 700 million years ago, when this part of the continent was near the Equator. This is one of several finds providing evidence that Earth underwent a 50-million-year period during which it was totally covered in ice. Dubbed, Snowball Earth, it may have been more like a slushball, with partially frozen, slushy oceans around the Equator. Life is thought to have survived in tiny pockets of unfrozen sea.

VOLCANOES

Volcanoes occur when a crack, or vent, in Earth's crust allows molten lava, volcanic ash, and hot gases to escape. The ash and rock collect around the vent to form cone-shaped mountains.

Clouds of ash and gas

Magma is molten rock below the surface. It has a temperature of about 2,700°F.

Crater

Main vent

Secondary vent

Layers of cooledf lava and ash

Magma collects near the surface in a magma chamber.

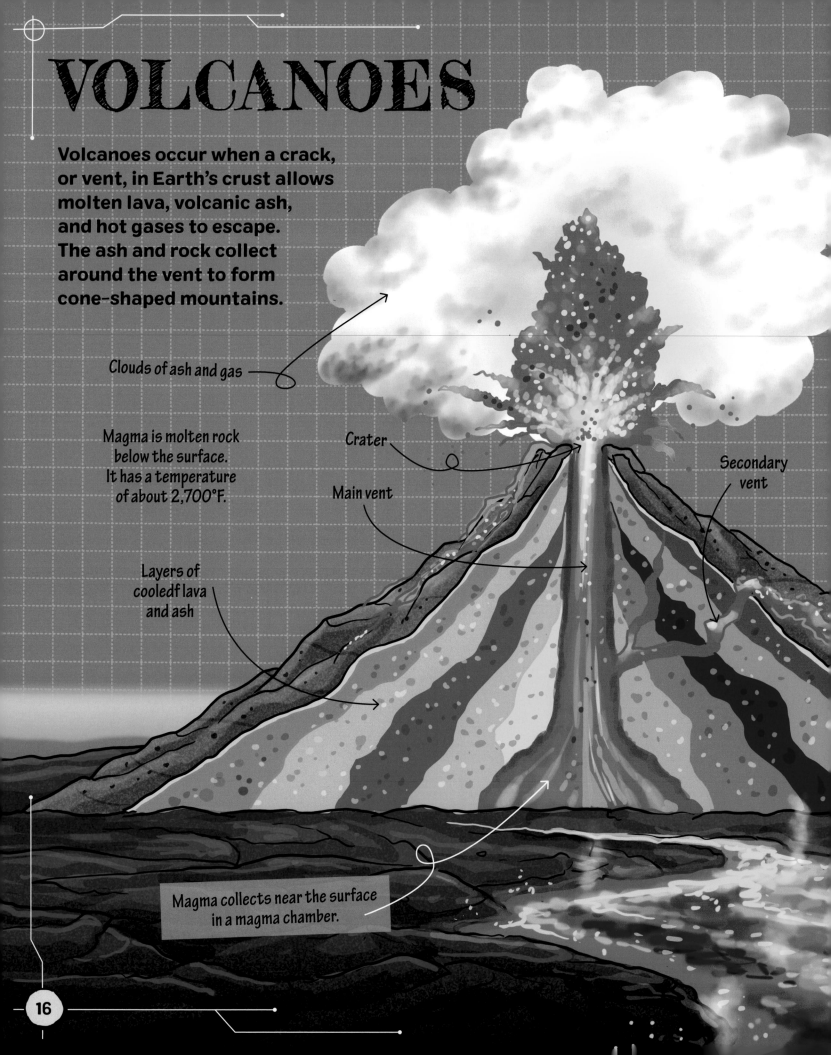

A new mountain

On February 20, 1943, farmers working in a cornfield in central Mexico noticed the field start to swell up underneath them. This was the start of a volcanic eruption that would last for the next nine years. By the end of the eruption, a 1,391-foot-high volcanic mountain called Parícutin stood on the land. The volcano gave scientists the unique opportunity to study a volcanic eruption through its entire lifecycle.

GEYSERS

Geysers are tube-like holes filled with water that extend deep into Earth's crust. They erupt periodically, sending jets of water and steam into the air. Old Faithful, a geyser in Yellowstone, Wyoming, is named after the regularity of its eruptions. It erupts about 20 times each day, sending water as high as 160 feet into the air.

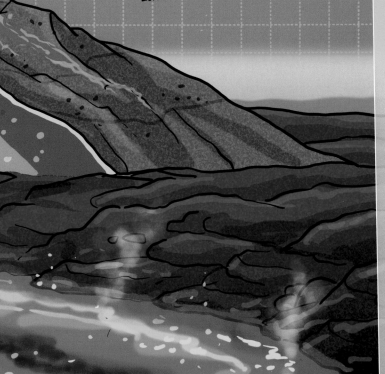

Lava

BURIED CITY

Mount Vesuvius in southern Italy is a very active volcano that has erupted many times. Its most destructive eruption occurred in 79 CE. The nearby city of Pompeii was buried under volcanic ash and rock. Archeologists have since uncovered much of the city, discovering casts made by the bodies of people who were buried alive by the ash.

EARTHQUAKES

Earthquakes are a violent shaking of Earth's surface. They are caused by sudden movements of the tectonic plates and occur most frequently at plate boundaries.

SHOCK WAVES

An earthquake causes shockwaves called seismic waves. There are three types:

P-waves

P-waves are longitudinal waves that move the rock forwards and backwards. They travel through the crust at a speed of about 4 miles per second.

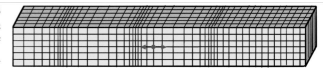

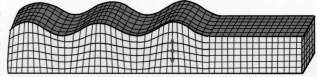

S-waves

These are transverse waves that move up and down or side to side, like the waves caused by dropping a stone in water. S-waves travel through the crust at about half the speed of P-waves.

Surface waves

These are transverse waves that travel near Earth's surface. They move more slowly than S-waves. Surface waves are often the most destructive type of seismic wave.

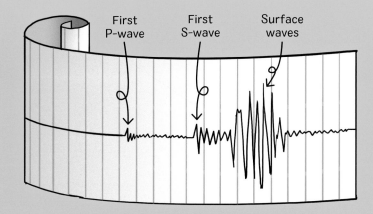

First P-wave   First S-wave   Surface waves

SEISMOGRAPHS

Earthquakes are measured using a seismometer, which records the seismic waves as a series of zig-zags on a seismograph. This seismometer recording shows the three kinds of wave arriving at different times. First the P-waves, then the S-waves, and finally the surface waves.

RICHTER AND GUTENBERG

US seismologists Beno Gutenberg (1889–1960) and Charles Richter (1900–1985) developed a scale now called the Richter scale to measure the size, or magnitude, of earthquakes. The scale is logarithmic, which means that a magnitude 6 earthquake is 10 times as strong as a magnitude 5. Earthquakes measuring from 1 to 5 on the Richter scale are relatively small and occur millions of times a year around the world. Highly destructive earthquakes measure more than 8 on the Richter scale and occur about once a year.

Beno Gutenberg   *Charles Richter*

GIANT WAVE

An earthquake under the ocean can create a giant wave called a tsunami. The tsunami spreads out from the center of the earthquake in all directions. Tsunamis can reach up to 100 feet tall and cause devastation when they hit land. They move at speeds of up to 500 mph, which is as fast as a jet plane. Tsunamis can travel thousands of miles across the oceans.

GREAT CHILE EARTHQUAKE

The most violent earthquake ever recorded was the Great Chile Earthquake in 1960, which measured 9.5 on the Richter scale. It sent tsunamis across the Pacific Ocean. The tsunamis hit the islands of Hawaii, 6,000 miles away, 15 hours after the earthquake.

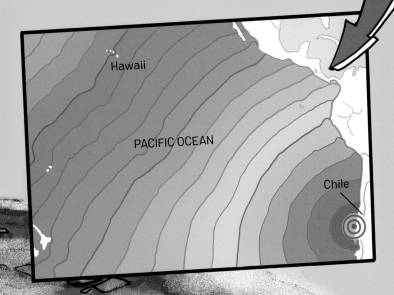

Hawaii

PACIFIC OCEAN

Chile

THE ROCK CYCLE

The rock cycle is a series of processes that create and destroy rock in Earth's crust.

1. Weathering and erosion
Rocks at the surface are weathered (worn away) by the wind and rain. Small particles such as pebbles and sand are carried into the oceans by rivers, glaciers, and the wind. This is called erosion.

2. Burial and compaction
The rock particles settle on the ocean bed as layers of sediment. The sediment is buried and compacted to form **sedimentary** rock.

3. Metamorphism
As Earth's crust slowly moves, rocks are placed under huge heat and pressure and transformed into **metamorphic** rock.

4. Melting
Rock melts deep underground to form magma.

5. Crystallization
As magma rises, it cools to form **igneous** rock.

Sandstone is a sedimentary rock formed of sand-sized grains.

Coal is a sedimentary rock formed of the remains of plants and animals.

Sedimentary rock

Slate is a metamorphic rock that splits easily into thin layers.

Metamorphic rock

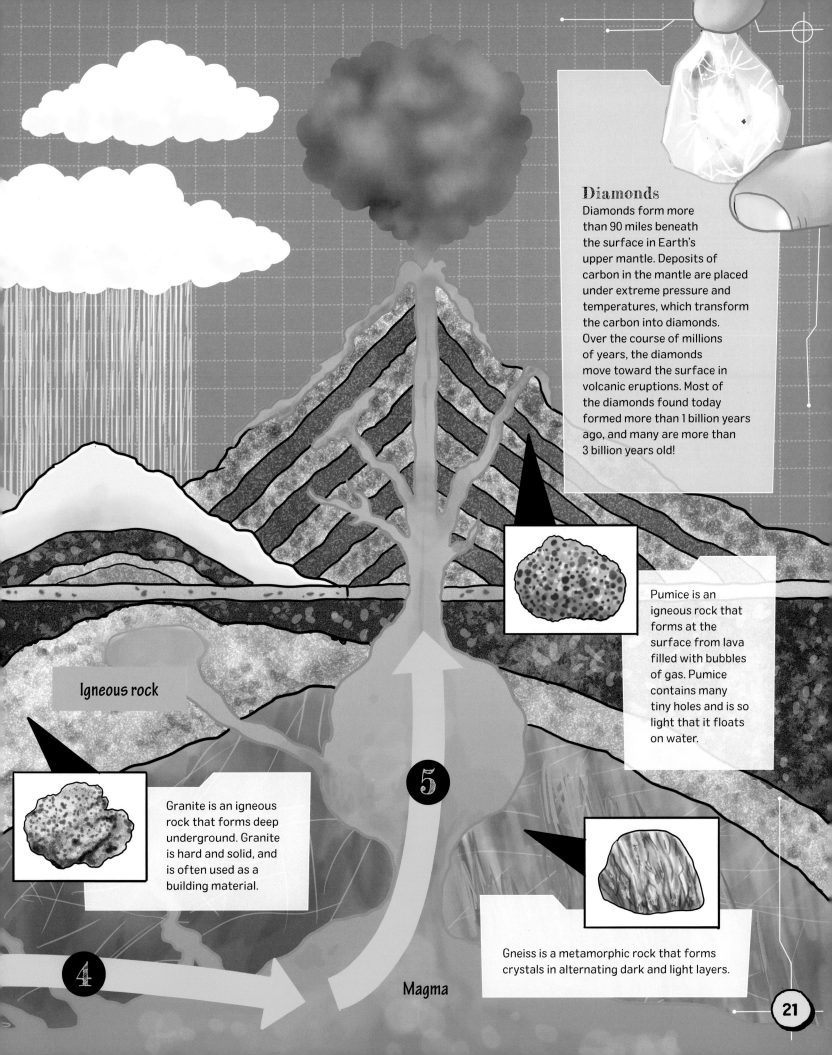

Diamonds

Diamonds form more than 90 miles beneath the surface in Earth's upper mantle. Deposits of carbon in the mantle are placed under extreme pressure and temperatures, which transform the carbon into diamonds. Over the course of millions of years, the diamonds move toward the surface in volcanic eruptions. Most of the diamonds found today formed more than 1 billion years ago, and many are more than 3 billion years old!

Pumice is an igneous rock that forms at the surface from lava filled with bubbles of gas. Pumice contains many tiny holes and is so light that it floats on water.

Igneous rock

Granite is an igneous rock that forms deep underground. Granite is hard and solid, and is often used as a building material.

Gneiss is a metamorphic rock that forms crystals in alternating dark and light layers.

Magma

CAVES

Cave systems form in rocks such as limestone that are water soluble. The resultant landscape is known as a karst landscape. It features caves, sinkholes, and underground rivers and lakes.

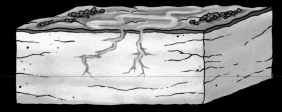

Water flows into cracks in the rocks.

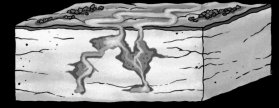

The underground current erodes the rock.

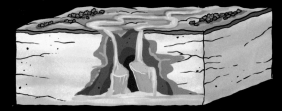

Large caves develop.

HOW CAVES FORM

Rainfall absorbs small amounts of carbon dioxide from the air and soil to form a weak carbonic acid. The acidic water flows into cracks in the rocks and dissolves small amounts of rock as it moves. Over the course of thousands of years, the cracks widen to form caves.

MINERAL COLUMNS

As water drips from the roofs of caves, it leaves behind small amounts of minerals such as calcium carbonate. Long, pointed stalactites grow from the roof, while broader stalagmites grow from the floor where the drops land. Over time, stalactites and stalagmites may join together in the middle to form columns.

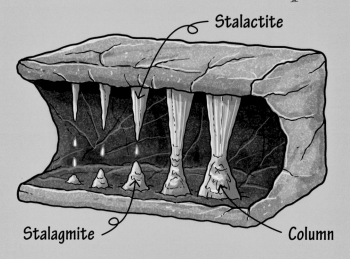

stalacTites grow from the Top

Stalactite

Stalagmite

Column

stalaGmites grow from the Ground

SINKHOLES

Sinkholes are found where the rocks above a cave have collapsed, creating a deep hole that often has a lake at the bottom.

The Red Lake in Croatia is a deep lake in the bottom of a sinkhole. The depth of the sinkhole is 1,700 feet from the rim. The lake is about 950 feet deep.

1,600 feet

1,700 feet

CAVE LABYRINTH

Mammoth Cave in Kentucky, USA, is the largest known cave system in the world. More than 420 miles of caves have been explored, and scientists think that another 600 miles remain to be discovered. The cave system started to form about 10 million years ago, and it continues to be slowly carved out by the water that flows through it.

THE GRAND CANYON

The Grand Canyon is a 277-mile-long valley in Arizona. The canyon has been carved through the rocks by the Colorado River over the course of the last 6 million years, exposing layers of rock that are nearly 2 billion years old.

HORSESHOE BEND

About 5 miles from the start of the Grand Canyon is the spectacular Horseshoe Bend. At this point, the river meanders and curves around on itself, carving out 1,000-foot-high cliffs. In the future, the river is likely to cut through the neck of the bend, abandoning the meander and creating a natural bridge.

A natural bridge will form in the future.

HIKING THROUGH TIME

At the top of the South Rim, you stand on rocks that are 270 million years old. Hikers on the South Kaibab trail work their way down from there to the river at the bottom of the canyon, where the Vishnu group formations are 1.68 billion years old. On the way, they pass through hundreds of millions of years of sedimentary rocks.

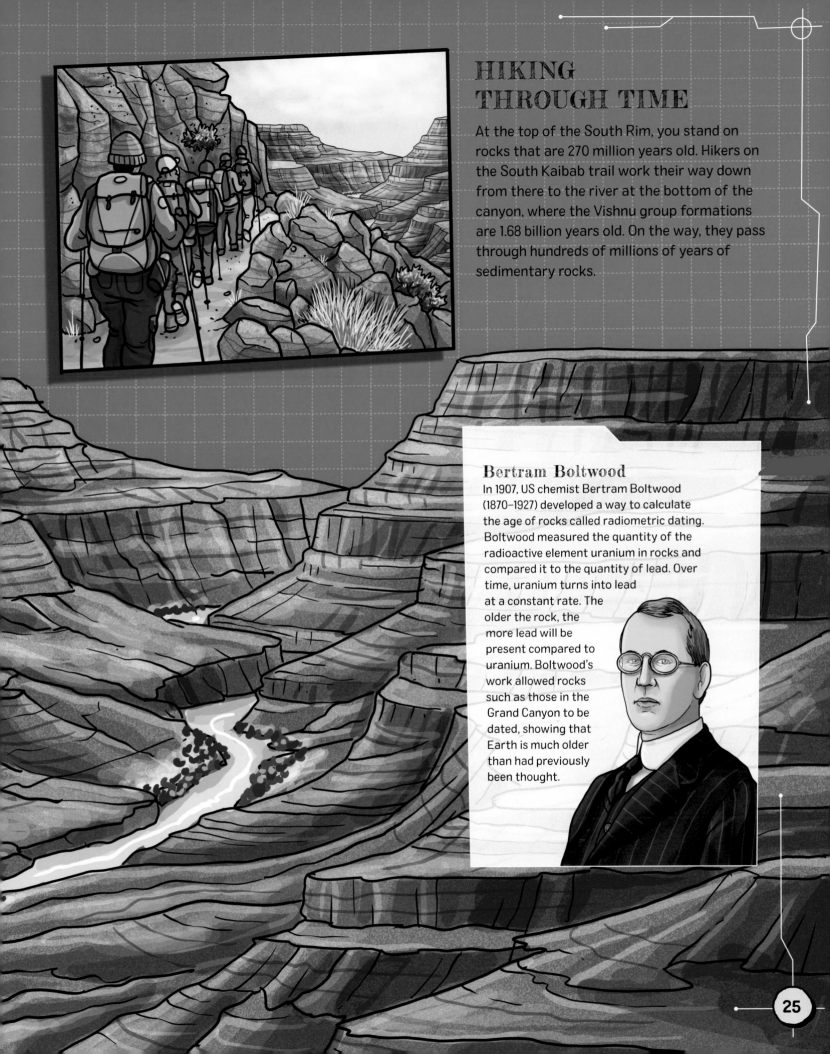

Bertram Boltwood

In 1907, US chemist Bertram Boltwood (1870–1927) developed a way to calculate the age of rocks called radiometric dating. Boltwood measured the quantity of the radioactive element uranium in rocks and compared it to the quantity of lead. Over time, uranium turns into lead at a constant rate. The older the rock, the more lead will be present compared to uranium. Boltwood's work allowed rocks such as those in the Grand Canyon to be dated, showing that Earth is much older than had previously been thought.

FOSSILS

Fossils are the preserved remains of ancient animals and plants. Scientists study the fossil record to reconstruct the history of life on Earth.

FORMING FOSSILS

Fossils are found in sedimentary rocks. The layer they are found in shows when they were alive.

1. Soon after it dies, an animal's body may be buried in sediment, such as volcanic ash or silt from rivers. The sediment prevents the bones from rotting.

2. Over time, more layers of sediment cover the remains and the calcium phosphate in the bones is replaced by minerals such as silica. The fossil is now encased in sedimentary rock.

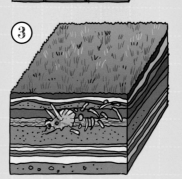

3. As tectonic plates move and rock layers deform, the fossil is pushed closer to the surface.

4. Erosion by water and wind wears away the rock, exposing the fossil at the surface.

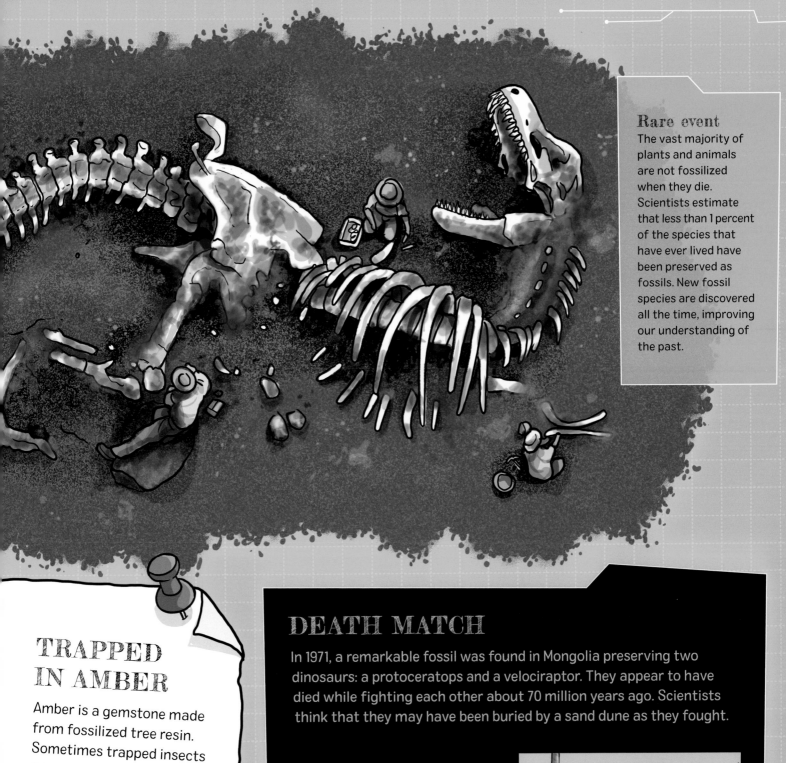

Rare event

The vast majority of plants and animals are not fossilized when they die. Scientists estimate that less than 1 percent of the species that have ever lived have been preserved as fossils. New fossil species are discovered all the time, improving our understanding of the past.

TRAPPED IN AMBER

Amber is a gemstone made from fossilized tree resin. Sometimes trapped insects are preserved inside amber. The largest concentration of amber is found on beaches around the Baltic Sea in Northern Europe. The insects trapped in Baltic amber lived between 35 and 50 million years ago.

DEATH MATCH

In 1971, a remarkable fossil was found in Mongolia preserving two dinosaurs: a protoceratops and a velociraptor. They appear to have died while fighting each other about 70 million years ago. Scientists think that they may have been buried by a sand dune as they fought.

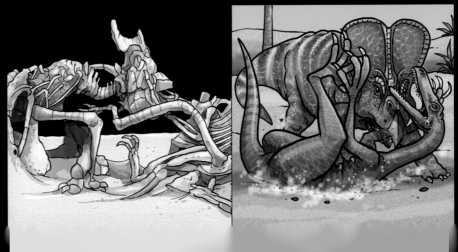

THE JURASSIC COAST

The Jurassic Coast is a 95-mile-long stretch of coastline in Southern England whose cliff-faces and beaches are rich in fossils. Every year, thousands of visitors explore the rocks in search of a precious find.

AGE OF DINOSAURS

Dinosaurs first appear in the fossil record in rocks that are 243 years old. Most of the dinosaurs disappeared in a mass extinction 66 million years ago. Only a few survived, becoming the ancestors of today's birds. The Jurassic Coast is the only place in the world with rocks that cover the whole of this period.

DINOSAUR FOOTPRINTS

More than 100 fossilized footprints have been preserved in a flat layer of rock in Keates Quarry on the Jurassic Coast. The footprints were made 140 million years ago by giant dinosaurs called sauropods. The large number of prints suggests that they may have gathered to drink at a watering hole. The prints they left in the mud were covered by layers of sediment and fossilized. They were discovered by quarry workers in 1997.

Sea life

Two hundred million years ago, this part of the land was near the Equator under a tropical sea. Fossils of ammonites, marine molluscs that lived around that time, are common.

MARY ANNING

Paleontologist Mary Anning (1799–1847) collected fossils around the town of Lyme Regis on the Jurassic Coast. Anning made detailed drawings of her finds, which greatly increased scientific understanding of the way species can go extinct. Among her key discoveries were an ichthyosaur and a plesiosaur, large marine reptiles. They lived about 200 million years ago, but that was not known at the time.

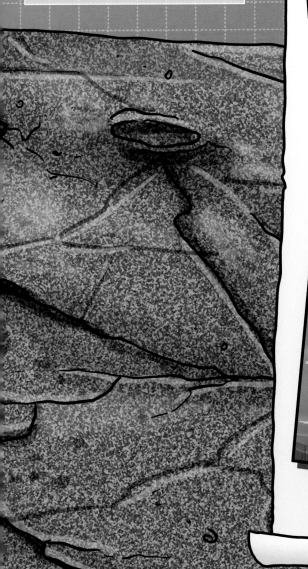

Anning drew the first complete skeleton of a plesiosaur. Despite her important discoveries, she struggled for recognition and relied on selling fossils to collectors to make ends meet.

WATERY PLANET

Water exists on Earth in three different states: solid, liquid, and gas. Water changes state and moves around the planet in a process called the water cycle.

96.5%
in the oceans

1.7%
in lakes, rivers, streams, and soil

1.7%
in polar ice caps, glaciers, and permanent snow

0.1%
as water vapor in the air

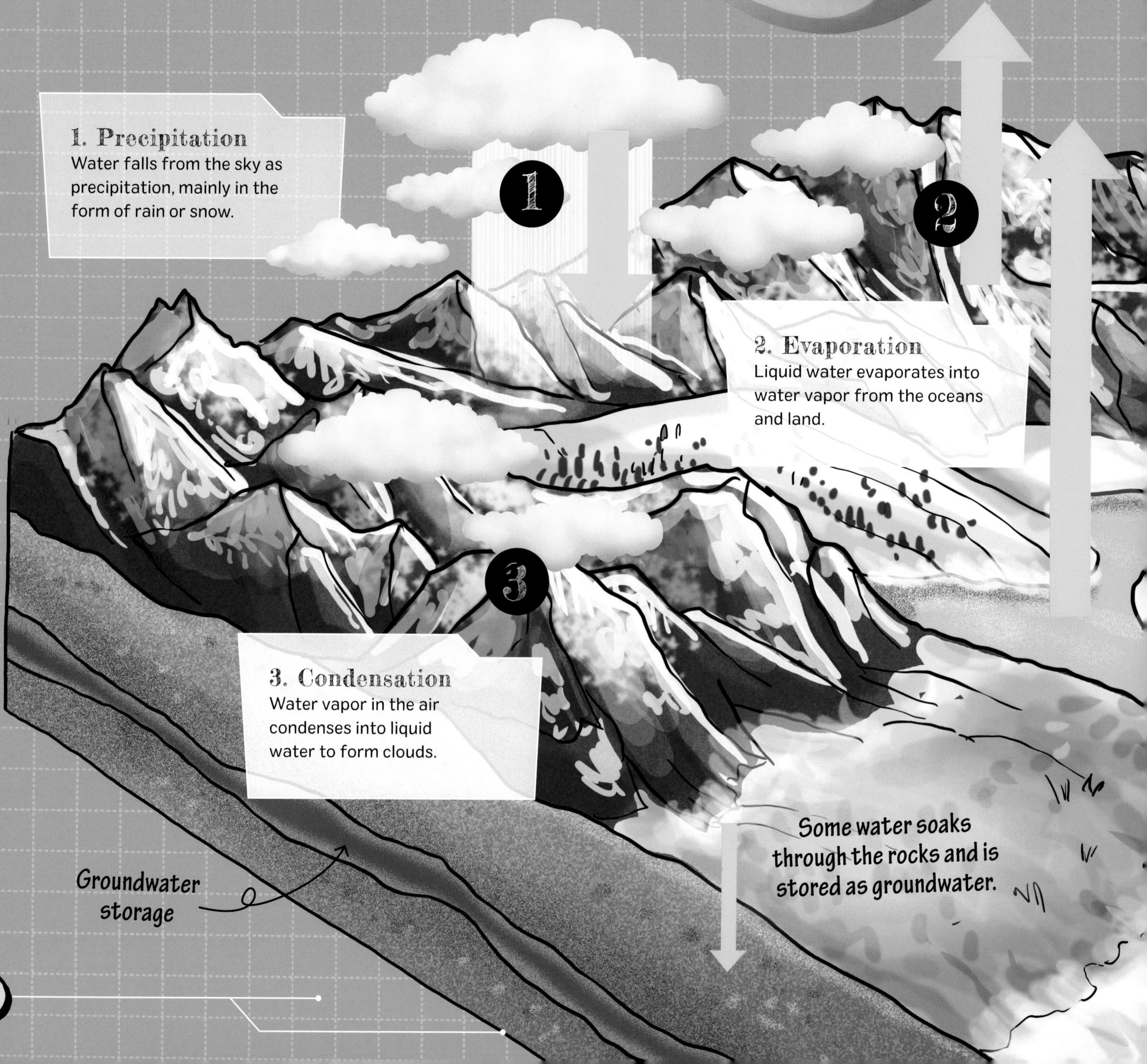

1. Precipitation
Water falls from the sky as precipitation, mainly in the form of rain or snow.

1

2

2. Evaporation
Liquid water evaporates into water vapor from the oceans and land.

3

3. Condensation
Water vapor in the air condenses into liquid water to form clouds.

Some water soaks through the rocks and is stored as groundwater.

Groundwater storage

Global conveyor belt

Water in the oceans moves in a set of currents known collectively as the global conveyor belt.

1. At the surface, winds create currents that carry water toward the poles.

2. Near the poles, the water cools, becoming more dense. Some of the water freezes, increasing the salinity (saltiness) of the remaining water and making it even more dense. The dense water sinks and spreads toward the Equator in deep currents.

3. The deep currents eventually rise back to the surface to start the process once again.

It takes a single drop of water about 1,000 years to complete a full cycle along the global conveyor belt.

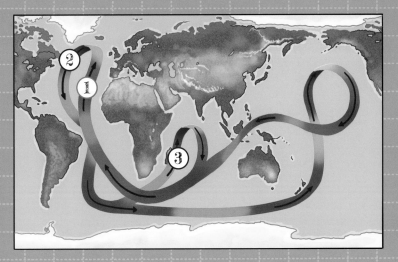

Antarctic ice sheet

Antarctica is covered in an ice sheet that is up to 3 miles thick. The ice sheet contains 90 percent of the world's ice and 70 percent of the world's fresh water. Scientists drill cores deep into the ice sheet and have discovered ice that is 2.7 million years old. The scientists study the chemical composition of the ancient ice to learn more about the history of Earth's climate.

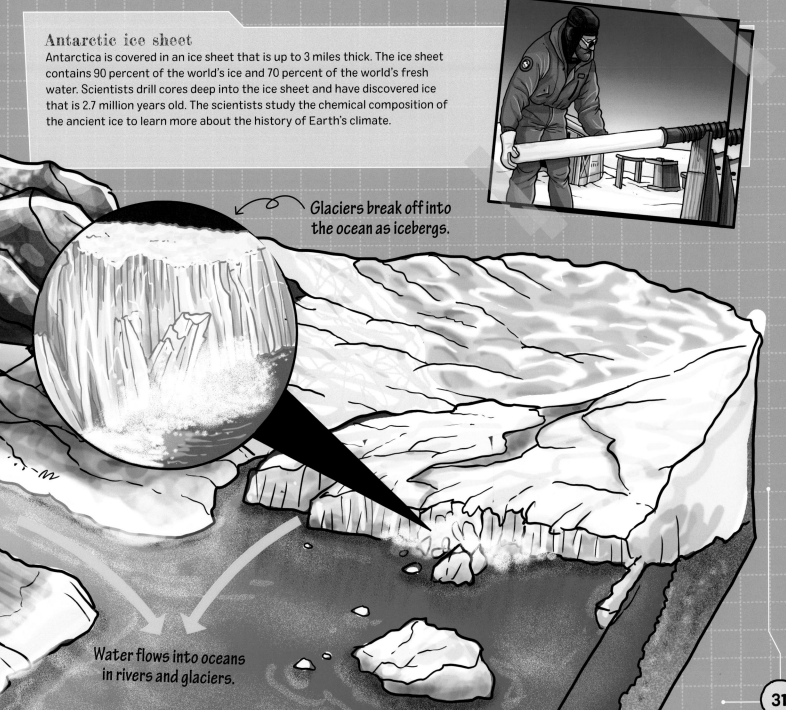

Glaciers break off into the ocean as icebergs.

Water flows into oceans in rivers and glaciers.

BLUE PLANET

From space, planet Earth appears blue. This is because 71 percent of the surface is covered in water.

SALTY OCEANS

Nearly 97 percent of the water on Earth is salt water. This is the water that makes up the oceans. The average depth of the world's oceans is 12,100 feet. The deepest point in the oceans is Challenger Deep in the Mariana Trench, at 36,000 feet. At this depth, the pressure is 1,000 times higher than atmospheric pressure—enough to instantly crush a human body.

Into the deep

In 1960, two intrepid explorers, Jacques Piccard and Don Walsh, descended to the bottom of Challenger Deep in a specially built deep-sea vessel called a bathyscaphe. The pair were protected from the extreme pressure inside a small sphere at the bottom of the vessel that provided everything needed for life support, like a spacecraft. They peered out of the sphere through small windows made of tough acrylic glass. In 2012, filmmaker James Cameron became the only other person to explore Challenger Deep.

Pacific Ocean

Mariana Trench

Challenger Deep

Amazon River

Digging for water

Groundwater collects deep underground in porous rocks and rock fractures. These are called aquifers. Aquifers can be reached by digging a well. In dry parts of the world, millions of people depend on wells to supply them with fresh water.

FRESH WATER

About 70 percent of the fresh water on Earth is frozen solid in the ice sheets at the poles. Most of the rest of the fresh water is found in the ground as either liquid or ice. Only about 0.3 percent of the world's fresh water is found in the surface water of lakes, rivers, and swamps.

Lake Baikal in Russia (above) is the deepest freshwater lake in the world. It is 5,387 feet deep and contains 20 percent of the world's liquid fresh water.

The Amazon River Delta (where it empties into the ocean), as seen from space

Water drains from land into the oceans along streams and rivers. The largest river in the world is the Amazon River (left), which flows through the Amazon rain forest and empties into the Atlantic Ocean. About 20 percent of all the fresh water that flows into the oceans passes through the Amazon, which is more than the next seven biggest rivers combined!

ATMOSPHERE

The atmosphere is layers of gas that surround Earth, held in place by Earth's gravity. Our planet's atmosphere contains the oxygen that is vital to life. It also protects us from the extreme radiation that comes from space.

ATMOSPHERIC LAYERS

As you move down through the atmosphere, you pass through a series of layers. The outer edge of the atmosphere is very thin and fades into interplanetary space. The air becomes thicker as you move toward the surface of the Earth.

The atmosphere is made from a mix of gases, including varying amounts of water vapor.

- **78%** Nitrogen
- **21%** Oxygen
- **1%** Other gases, including argon, carbon dioxide, and water vapor

EXOSPHERE
300 miles to 2,000 miles

The exosphere is the top layer and extends thousands of miles up. The air in this layer is very thin. The exosphere does not have a sharp edge to it, but fades gradually into space the higher you go.

GPS satellites orbit Earth in the exosphere.

Hubble Space Telescope

THERMOSPHERE
50 miles to 300 miles

The International Space Station (ISS) orbits Earth in the thermosphere. While the atmosphere is very hot here, it is also very thin so it does not damage the ISS.

The thermosphere extends above the mesosphere up to 300 miles. This part of the atmosphere is bombarded with X-rays and ultraviolet light from space and the temperature can reach more than 1,800°F.

Auroras form in the thermosphere (see page 37).

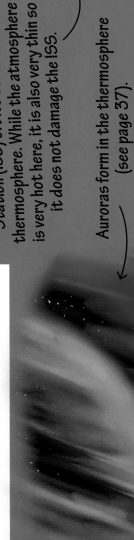

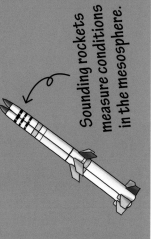

Sounding rockets measure conditions in the mesosphere.

The mesosphere extends above the stratosphere to about 50 miles. Temperatures fall as you rise through the mesosphere, from 27.5°F to –123°F.

MESOSPHERE
30 miles to 50 miles

Meteors burn up in the mesosphere, creating shooting stars.

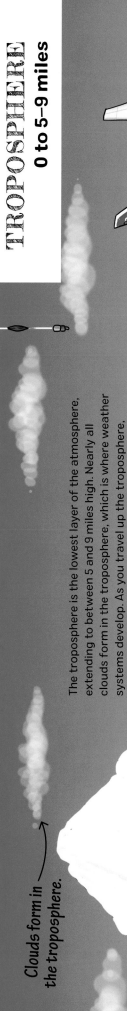

STRATOSPHERE
5–9 miles to 30 miles

The stratosphere extends from the edge of the troposphere to about 30 miles. The stratosphere contains the ozone layer, which protects us from damaging ultraviolet light from the Sun. The ozone layer causes the temperature to rise through the stratosphere, from –69°F at the bottom to 27.5°F at the top.

Weather balloons send back information from the stratosphere.

TROPOSPHERE
0 to 5–9 miles

The troposphere is the lowest layer of the atmosphere, extending to between 5 and 9 miles high. Nearly all clouds form in the troposphere, which is where weather systems develop. As you travel up the troposphere, the average temperature falls from 59°F to –69°F.

Clouds form in the troposphere.

MAGNETIC PLANET

Earth's magnetic field runs from the north magnetic pole to the south magnetic pole.

Earth is a giant magnet, surrounded by an invisible magnetic field called the magnetosphere. The magnetosphere protects us from harmful radiation emitted by the Sun.

MOVING POLES

Earth's magnetism is created by the movement of liquid iron in the outer core. Changes in the direction of the currents of iron cause the magnetic poles to move. The magnetic north pole is currently moving at about 34 miles per year. Navigation equipment that relies on magnetism needs to be updated regularly to account for this change.

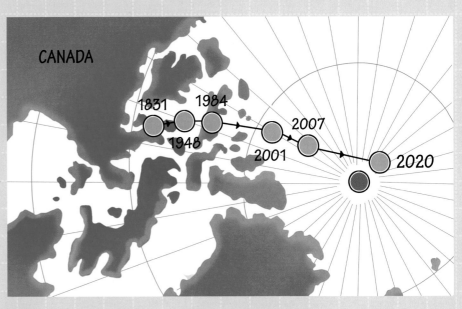

CANADA

1831 1984
1948
2001 2007
2020

⬤ Magnetic North Pole   ⬤ Geographical North Pole (the northern point on Earth's axis of rotation, see page 5).

GLOWING SKIES

The magnetosphere acts like an invisible shield, protecting us from charged particles that stream out from the Sun. Most of the charged particles are deflected by the magnetosphere, but some are captured by it and move along the magnetic field into the atmosphere around the poles. The charged particles interact with the gases in the atmosphere to produce a spectacular display of glowing colors called an aurora.

Navigating by magnetism

The beaks of some birds, such as pigeons, contain a magnetic mineral called magnetite. This allows them to sense the magnetosphere, which they use to navigate. The birds may also be able to see the magnetosphere using special cells in their eyes.

Magnetite

STORMY PLANET

Towering storm clouds can extend upward from low altitudes all the way to the edge of the troposphere. These giant clouds are a sure sign of severe weather heading your way.

TROPICAL CYCLONE

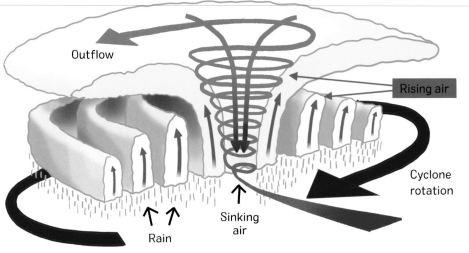

Outflow

Rising air

Cyclone rotation

Rain

Sinking air

Tropical cyclones, also known as hurricanes or typhoons, are storms that form over tropical oceans. These huge rotating masses of cloud can wreak destruction when they hit land, with winds of more than 125 mph. Satellites monitor tropical cyclones from space, providing early warnings where the storms are going to hit land.

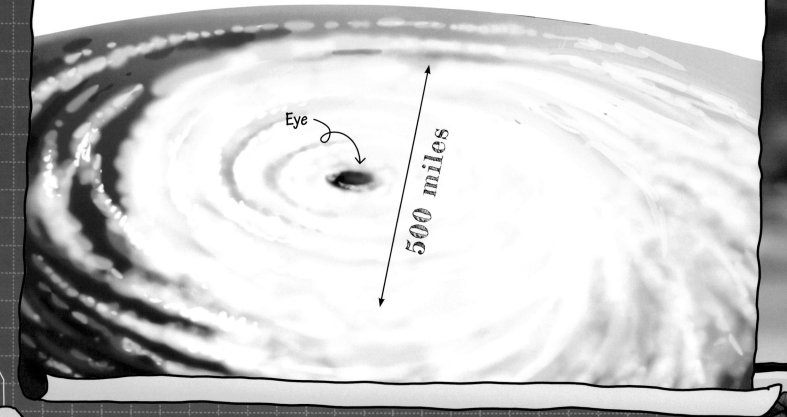

Eye

500 miles

TWISTERS

Tornadoes, or twisters, are violently rotating columns of air that stretch from the bottom of a storm cloud to the ground. Winds inside a tornado can reach more than 185 mph, flattening anything in their path.

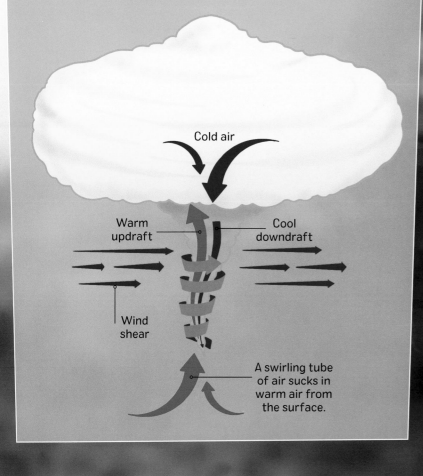

Cold air

Warm updraft

Cool downdraft

Wind shear

A swirling tube of air sucks in warm air from the surface.

VIOLENT SKIES

Storms are not the only way that destruction can come from the skies.

LIGHTNING

Lightning is a giant spark of electricity that passes through the air between clouds or between clouds and the ground. The air along a narrow channel is briefly heated to 54,000°F—hotter than the surface of the Sun! A flash of lightning lasts just 0.2 seconds, but it contains a huge amount of energy. The air explodes outward, causing a shock wave that we hear as thunder.

Count the seconds

When you see lightning, the flash reaches you almost straight away as it travels at the speed of light (186,000 miles per second). However, thunder travels through the air at the speed of sound, which is much slower—about 1,100 feet per second. To work out how far away a lightning strike was from you, count the number of seconds between seeing the strike and hearing the thunder. Every five seconds equal one mile.

What causes lightning

Lightning occurs when positive electric charge builds up at the top of thunderclouds and negative charge at the bottom. This causes an area of positive charge to build up on the ground. Once the difference between the two charges is large enough, negatively charged electrons flow from the cloud to the ground. Positive charge flows from the ground to the cloud, and this is what we see as the flash of lightning.

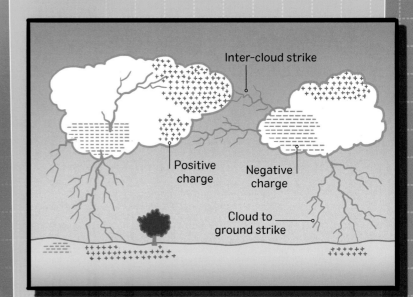

Inter-cloud strike

Positive charge

Negative charge

Cloud to ground strike

HAILSTONES

Hailstones are balls of solid ice that form high in storm clouds. Inside very large clouds, hailstones can grow to huge sizes. The largest hailstone ever measured fell on South Dakota, in 2010. It was 8 inches in diameter and weighed almost 2 pounds. Falling at more than 60 mph, large hailstones such as this can be deadly.

Raining frogs?

On extremely rare occasions, storms have been reported in which thousands of frogs have fallen from the sky. Scientists think that frogs may be sucked up into clouds by tornadoes passing over lakes and ponds. They are then deposited back to the ground all at once many miles away.

Wall of sand

Sandstorms are common in many deserts. Huge sandstorms called haboobs form in strong winds that blow down from storm clouds. The winds collect sand and dust from the ground to form a dense wall that can reach a height of more than 3,000 feet. Haboobs move at up to 60 mph and can appear with very little warning. It may take up to 3 hours for the storm to pass.

CLIMATE CHANGE

Earth's climate (its long-term weather pattern) has changed dramatically over its 4.5 billion-year life for a variety of reasons. However, in the last century, the climate has been warming rapidly due to human activity. We urgently need to put in place measures to stop this global heating.

THE GREENHOUSE EFFECT

The planet is warming because we are placing more greenhouse gases into the atmosphere. Greenhouse gases, such as carbon dioxide and methane, absorb heat radiated by the ground rather than allowing it to escape into space. The heat is re-emitted in all directions, warming the surface and lower atmosphere.

ATMOSPHERE

Reflected light

INFRARED RADIATION (HEAT)

RADIATION FROM THE SUN

Heat absorbed by greenhouse gases and emitted back to Earth

Radiation absorbed by the surface and given off as heat

BURNING FOSSIL FUELS

Fossil fuels are substances such as oil and coal made from the remains of ancient plants and animals that were buried in Earth's crust. The carbon in fossil fuels has been locked away underground for millions of years. When we burn these fuels, we release a lot of carbon dioxide into the atmosphere in a relatively short time. In the past 200 years, the level of carbon dioxide in the atmosphere has increased by 50 percent.

Disappearing ice

The average global temperature has increased by 2°F in the past 50 years. This has caused the ice around the poles to shrink in size. Around the North Pole, Arctic sea ice reaches its minimum extent each September. This September minimum is shrinking at a rate of 12.5 percent per decade.

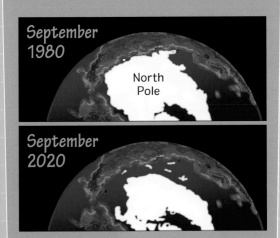

September 1980

North Pole

September 2020

CARBON CAPTURE

Some scientists are working on radical solutions to climate change, such as using technology to take carbon dioxide out of the atmosphere. One proposed solution is called direct air capture. Carbon dioxide (CO_2) is captured from the air and placed deep underground. This reverses the process by which fossil fuels were mined from the ground.

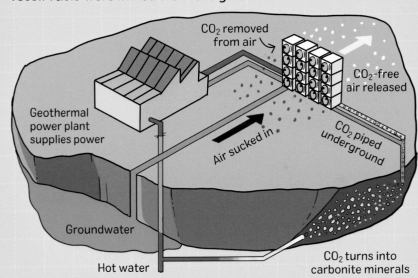

CO_2 removed from air

CO_2-free air released

Geothermal power plant supplies power

Air sucked in

CO_2 piped underground

Groundwater

Hot water

CO_2 turns into carbonite minerals

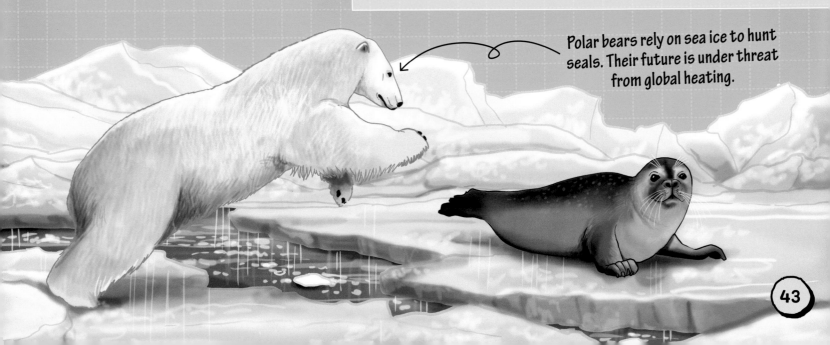

Polar bears rely on sea ice to hunt seals. Their future is under threat from global heating.

FUTURE PLANET

In the coming decades, we face the challenge of adapting to a changing planet and stopping global heating. Looking further into the future, millions of years from now, Earth will look very different from today as a result of the immense forces that are constantly at work shaping and reshaping our world.

WHAT CAN WE DO?

Tackling global heating is one of the biggest challenges we face in the 21st century.

We need to recycle our waste as much as possible. The energy saved by recycling just one glass bottle is enough to power a computer for 25 minutes.

We need to change over to renewable energy sources such as solar, wind, or hydroelectric.

We need to reduce the amount that we drive cars or fly in aircraft by using greener travel, such as trains powered by electricity.

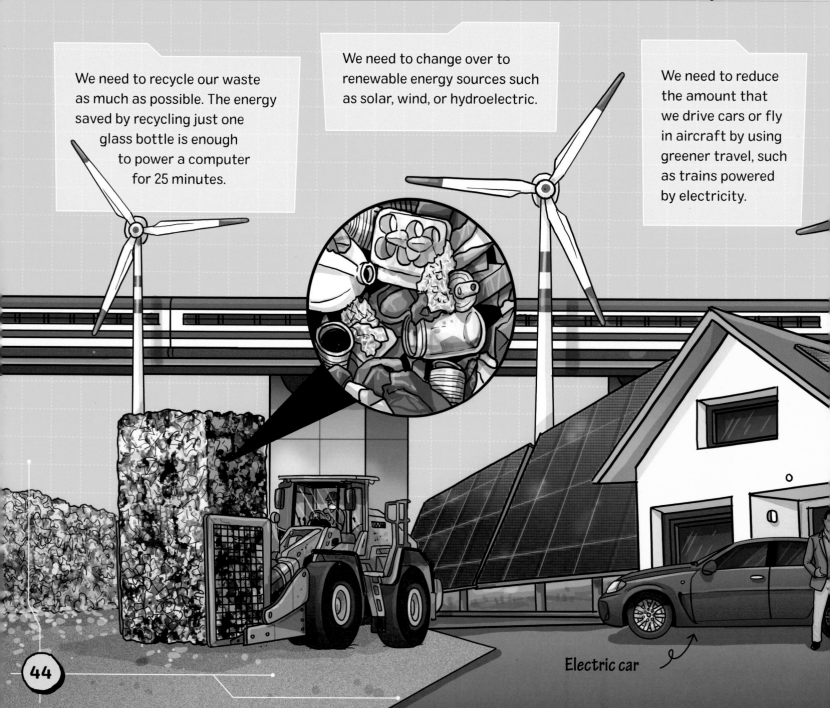

Electric car

44

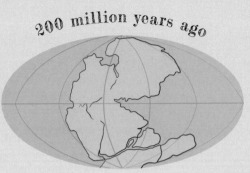
200 million years ago

Present day

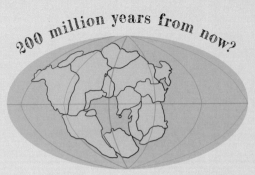
200 million years from now?

A NEW PANGAEA

Two hundred million years ago, all of Earth's land was joined together as a supercontinent called Pangaea. This broke up to form today's continents. The continents continue to move, and in about 200 million years' time, scientists predict that they will come together to form a new supercontinent.

We need to insulate homes so that they use energy efficiently.

Plants take carbon dioxide from the atmosphere. We need to protect the world's forests, which absorb billions of tons of carbon dioxide each year.

GLOSSARY

atmospheric pressure
The pressure produced by the weight of the atmosphere. Atmospheric pressure reduces as you move up through the atmosphere.

aurora
A spectacular light display seen near the poles when charged particles from the Sun interact with Earth's atmosphere.

axis
An imaginary line around which a body such as Earth rotates.

charged particle
A particle with either a positive or a negative electric charge. Electrons are charged particles with negative charge. Ions are atoms or molecules with a positive or negative charge.

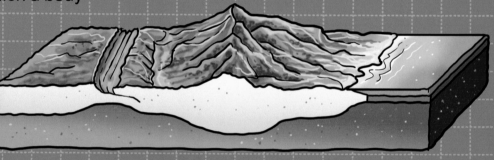

climate
The long-term patterns of weather in a particular area. Measured over many years, an area's climate includes measurements such as temperature or rainfall.

condensation
The change of a gas into a liquid. Water vapour in the atmosphere condenses to form clouds of water droplets.

eon
A very long unit of geological time, lasting up to 2 billion years. Geologists divide Earth's history into four eons. The current eon is called the Phanerozoic Eon.

electron
A tiny negatively charged particle.

evaporation
The change of a liquid into a gas, such as liquid water into water vapour.

evolution
The process by which living things change gradually over the course of many generations. When conditions on Earth change, life forms evolve that are better adapted to the new conditions.

lava
The molten rock that reaches Earth's surface through volcanoes.

limestone
A sedimentary rock formed from animal remains such as shells or coral. Limestone is mostly formed of the mineral calcium carbonate.

magnetic field

An area around a magnet in which a magnetic force can be felt. Earth is surrounded by a magnetic field that extends 40,000 miles into space.

methane

A chemical found in Earth's atmosphere. It is a greenhouse gas and increasing levels of methane in the atmosphere are contributing to global heating.

meteor

A small piece of rock or metal that burns brightly as it enters Earth's atmosphere from space.

molecule

A group of atoms that are bonded together. Molecules form the smallest units of chemical compounds.

oxygen

A gas that makes up about one-fifth of Earth's atmosphere. Oxygen is essential to life as it allows living things to turn their food into energy.

plateau

(pl. plateaux) An area of high, flat ground.

precipitation

Liquid or frozen water that falls from clouds in the form of rain, snow, or hail.

radiation

Energy that travels through space in the form of electromagnetic waves or charged particles. Visible light is a form of radiation.

radioactive element

An element made from atoms with unstable nuclei. Over time, the atoms decay, giving off radiation. This changes the atoms into a different element.

resin

A sticky substance produced by trees and other plants.

river delta

A triangular area of wetlands that forms where a river flows into the ocean, a lake, or another river.

satellite

An object that orbits a larger object such as a planet or a star, held in orbit by the force of gravity. The Moon is Earth's only natural satellite.

species

A group of closely related life forms that share similar characteristics and are able to reproduce with one another.

weathering

The geological process by which the surfaces of rocks or soil are gradually worn away by moving water, wind, or rain.

INDEX